I0820962

HORSE BREEDS

AMERICAN PAINT HORSE

BY WHITNEY SANDERSON

Kids Core

An Imprint of Abdo Publishing
abdobooks.com

abdobooks.com

Printed in the United States of America, North Mankato, Minnesota.
052025
092025

Cover Photo: Rita Kochmarjova/Shutterstock Images
Interior Photos: Tom McGinty/Shutterstock Images, 4–5; iStockphoto, 7, 9, 20–21, 23 (top left), 23 (top right), 23 (bottom); Julia Christe/fStop/Getty Images, 10; Rita Kochmarjova/Shutterstock Images, 12–13; Grafissimo/DigitalVision Vectors/Getty Images, 15; MPI/Archive Photos/Getty Images, 16; MoMo Productions/DigitalVision/Getty Images, 17; Shutterstock Images, 18, 25, 28–29; catnap/Alamy, 26

Editor: Marie Pearson
Series Designer: Ryan Gale

Library of Congress Control Number: 2024949082

Publisher's Cataloging-in-Publication Data

Names: Sanderson, Whitney, author.
Title: American paint horse / by Whitney Sanderson
Description: Minneapolis, Minnesota: Abdo Publishing, 2026 | Series: Horse breeds | Includes online resources and index.
Identifiers: ISBN 9781098297466 (lib. bdg.) | ISBN 9798384919988 (ebook)
Subjects: LCSH: American paint horse--Juvenile literature. | Horses--Juvenile literature. | Horse breeds--Juvenile literature. | Zoology--Juvenile literature.
Classification: DDC 636.13--dc23

CONTENTS

Riders try to turn their horses as tightly around each barrel as they can to get a fast run.

CHAPTER 1

BARREL RACING STAR

Flash shifted in place at the starting line, waiting for Ida's signal. His brown-and-white splashed coat glowed in the sunlight. The buzzer sounded. Ida and Flash took off toward the first of three barrels. The barrels were set in a triangular pattern.

The pair raced to circle each barrel in a cloverleaf pattern. They rounded the right barrel first. Ida laid the reins against the left side of Flash's neck so he would turn away from the pressure. She held her right leg steady against his side. That helped him turn tightly around the barrel without hitting it.

They made a left turn around the left barrel, then headed for the far barrel. The toe of Ida's right boot bumped against the third barrel as they circled it to the left. It wobbled. If it fell, it would add a penalty of five seconds to their time. But she couldn't watch to see if it fell. They had to get back to the finish line fast.

Now they had a straight path to the finish line. Ida leaned forward and urged Flash into

Rodeos are based on ranch work. The American paint horse can help ranchers move cattle.

his fastest gallop. They crossed the finish line! Ida sat deep in the saddle, and Flash slid to a stop.

She looked back to see if the last barrel was still standing. It was! The announcer said, "That's our best time tonight, 16.5 seconds!" Ida leaned down to hug Flash's neck. To her, nothing was more exciting than riding a barrel course on her speedy paint horse.

Hollywood Horses

The 2004 movie *Hidalgo* tells the story of a 3,000-mile (4,830-km) endurance race across the Arabian Desert in the Middle East. The horse in the movie is played by five American paint horses, who were each filmed in different scenes. Since paint horses have unique patterns, it was a challenge to find five similar horses!

Like other horses, paint horses should be kept in herds so they don't get lonely.

A Colorful Breed

The American paint horse is a breed known for its colorful coat patterns. Paint horses have patches of white mixed with nearly any color a horse can be. Paints are also smart, sturdy horses that work on ranches and compete in many types of riding sports.

Many people ride their paint horses for fun.

The paint is a popular breed. More than 1 million paint horses have been **registered** in 59 countries. They add a splash of color and plenty of talent to whatever they do.

In a *Horse Illustrated* magazine article, Kenli Marvin talks about a paint horse named Keeper:

> I love the uniqueness that comes with the paint horse, and I feel like they have a little extra "try" to them. Keeper definitely has the heart and the try, and she's just a gorgeous **mare**.

Source: Abigail Boatwright. "The American Paint Horse." *Horse Illustrated*, 19 May 2021, horseillustrated.com. Accessed 18 Dec. 2024.

Comparing Texts

Think about the quote. Does it support the information in the chapter? Or does it give a different perspective? Explain how in a few sentences.

People have admired pinto-colored horses for a long time.

CHAPTER 2

HISTORY OF THE AMERICAN PAINT

Horses with white-splashed coats have existed for thousands of years. This pattern is called pinto. Paintings from the 300s BCE in ancient Egypt show pinto horses. So does art from ancient China and India.

Pinto horses were often found in Spain. They were valued by wealthy people. When Spanish explorers came to the Americas in the 1500s, they brought horses with them. Some were pintos.

A few Spanish horses escaped to form wild herds. American Indians caught some of them. American Indians also traded for horses with the Spanish. The Comanche (Nʉmʉnʉʉ) people of the Southern Plains especially prized pinto horses.

Going West

In the 1840s, many settlers from the eastern part of the United States moved west. Cowboys raised cattle to ship to cities back east.

Artist Frederic Sackrider Remington drew a Comanche on a pinto horse in the 1890s.

They used ranch horses to get their work done. These horses became the American quarter horse breed. Sometimes, quarter horses had pinto foals.

Wild West shows were traveling performances of sharpshooting, trick riding, and acting that were popular in the late 1800s to early 1900s.

Some cowboys did not like these colorful patterns. They thought pinto horses weren't as good as solid-colored horses. They sold them to Wild West shows or circuses.

Ranchers still use pinto horses today.

But other ranchers liked the colorful horses. They realized that pinto horses were just as strong as horses of other colors. They were as fast too.

Speedy Paints

Races for paint horses started in 1966. Before that, paints raced with quarter horses. In the 1940s, a **stallion** named Painted Joe won three races against a famous quarter horse, Grey Badger II.

Some people own farms where they breed American paint horses.

Sometimes Thoroughbred racehorses were born with pinto coloring too. People began breeding pinto quarter horses and

Thoroughbreds on purpose. The offspring became the American paint horse breed.

The American Paint Horse Association formed in 1962 in Texas. It keeps a registry of all paint horses. It has horse shows just for paints. A foal can be registered if it has one paint parent and one Thoroughbred or quarter horse parent, as long as the foal has a pinto pattern.

Further Evidence

Look at the website below. Does it give any new evidence to support Chapter Two?

American Paint Horse

abdocorelibrary.com/american-paint-horse

Children can learn show jumping on paint horses.

CHAPTER 3

LIVING WITH THE AMERICAN PAINT

Paints are medium-sized, athletic horses. They are usually 14.2 to 16.2 hands tall at the shoulder. A hand is 4 inches (10 cm). Paints weigh 1,000 to 1,200 pounds (450–540 kg).

Paints are light horses. This means they are used for riding rather than pulling heavy loads.

Paints come in nearly every color a horse can be. Their white patches might combine with black, **palomino**, **buckskin**, shades of brown, or another color. Paint horses must have a white or colored marking at least 2 inches (5 cm) big on their body. Many paints have white stockings that go up above their knees or **hocks**. They often have white face markings.

Some horses with paint parents are born without the pinto pattern. They can be registered as a solid paint-bred horse. They can compete in paint horse shows and be used for breeding.

Paint Horse Patterns

Overero

The white does not cross the horse's back. The patches can have rough or smooth edges. The horse's face is often white.

Tobiano

The white crosses over the horse's back, and the body has smooth patches of color. The mane and tail are often a mix of white and color. The head is dark, sometimes with markings like solid-colored horses have.

Tovero

A combination of overo and tobiano, such as tobiano body coloring with a white face seen in the overo pattern.

Paint horses come in three basic coat patterns.

All-Around Athletes

Paint horses compete in many sports. They are most often seen in Western riding events such as cutting. In this sport, a horse and rider try to separate, or cut, a single cow from a herd.

A horse and rider must have good communication to do well in cutting. A horse also needs to have an instinct for how cows act.

Cinderella Story

In 2014, Kenli Marvin bid on a chestnut-and-white paint foal at an auction. When the bidding got too high, her father loaned her the rest of the money. The foal, Cinderella Cat, became a star cutting horse. By the time the horse was four years old, they had won $64,098 in prize money together!

Children can learn to take care of their paint horses.

This instinct is called "cow sense." Paint horses often have this talent.

People also ride paints just for fun. Paints are steady trail horses. They do well in English events, such as **dressage** and jumping. Their friendly, calm temperament makes them great for children and beginner riders.

Pole bending is a race where the horse and rider weave through a line of six poles and then back in a keyhole pattern.

Young riders with paint horses might compete in gymkhana. This contest has mounted games that test a horse's speed and **agility** and a rider's skill. Gymkhana games include pole bending and even an egg race where riders race to cross the finish line with an egg balanced on a spoon!

The paint horse is an American breed. It is easy to see why ancient people were drawn to these colorful horses. The horses' beauty and talent are why people still love them today.

Explore Online

Visit the website below. Does it give any new information about American paint horses that wasn't in Chapter Three?

Colors of the American Paint Horse

abdocorelibrary.com/american-paint-horse

BREED TRAITS

Powerful hindquarters

Solid, muscular body and legs

Often two-tone mane and tail
Narrow, straight head
Coat that is a mix of white and another color

Glossary

agility
the ability to start, turn, and stop quickly

buckskin
a tan or gold coat color with a black mane and tail

dressage
a sport in which a horse and rider perform graceful patterns with very small cues from the rider

hocks
the joints in the middle of a horse's hind legs, similar to human ankles

mare
a female horse

palomino
a gold coat color with a white mane and tail

registered
listed as a member of an organization

stallion
a male horse who can have offspring

Online Resources

To learn more about American paint horses and other horses, visit our free resource websites below.

Visit **abdocorelibrary.com** or scan this QR code for free Common Core resources for teachers and students, including vetted activities, multimedia, and booklinks, for deeper subject comprehension.

Visit **abdobooklinks.com** or scan this QR code for free additional online weblinks for further learning. These links are routinely monitored and updated to provide the most current information available.

Learn More

My Book of Horses and Ponies. DK, 2024.

Pearson, Marie. *Horse Behavior.* Abdo, 2024.

Ventura, Marne. *Horses.* Abdo, 2023.

Index

About the Author

Whitney Sanderson grew up riding horses as a member of a 4-H club and competing in local horse shows. She is the author of numerous children's books.